"THE WILD OLD WICKED MAN"
& OTHER POEMS

Also by Archibald MacLeish

Poems

Collected Poems, 1917–1952
Songs for Eve

Plays in Verse

Panic
The Fall of the City
Air Raid
The Trojan Horse
This Music Crept by Me upon the Waters
J.B.
Herakles

Prose

The Irresponsibles
The American Cause
A Time to Speak
A Time to Act
American Opinion and the War
Poetry and Opinion
Freedom Is the Right to Choose
Poetry and Experience
The Eleanor Roosevelt Story
A Continuing Journey

"THE WILD OLD
WICKED MAN"
& OTHER POEMS

by ARCHIBALD MacLEISH

HOUGHTON MIFFLIN COMPANY

BOSTON · 1968

First Printing w

Certain of the poems in this volume have appeared previously in various magazines, as follows:

"The Boatmen of Santorin": published in the Program for the Library Dedication Exercises at the University of Utah, May 17, 1968.

"Where a Poet's From": published in *Saturday Review*, November 28, 1967, © 1967 by Saturday Review, Inc.

"Cummings": published under the title "The Sunset" in *The Yale Literary Magazine*, September 1966.

"Hemingway": published under the title "The Gunshot" in *The Atlantic*, Copyright © 1961, by The Atlantic Monthly Company.

"Brooks Atkinson": published in *Equity*, September, 1960, Copyright 1960. Actors' Equity Association.

"How the River Ninfa Runs Through the Ruined Town Beneath the Lime Quarry": published in *Botteghe Oscure* in 1953.

"Contemporary Portrait": published in *The New Republic*, November 14, 1954.

"Hotel Breakfast": published in the *Chicago Tribune*, © 1967 Chicago Tribune.

"The Wild Old Wicked Man," "Black Humor," "Hurricane," "Waking," and "Boy in the Roman Zoo": published in *Saturday Review*, September, 1968, © 1968 by Saturday Review, Inc.

"Observations of P. Ovidius Naso on the Incidence of Sex in the Contemporary Novel": published in *Harper's*, September, 1968.

CONTENTS

Hurricane   1

The Ship in the Tomb   2

Creator   3

The Boatmen of Santorin   4

The Peepers in Our Meadow   5

Waking   6

Autobiography   7

Revolution of the Children   8

Black Humor   9

Boy in the Roman Zoo   10

Seeing   11

Companions   16

Survivor   17

Great Contemporary Discoveries   18

Spring in These Hills   20

Observations of P. Ovidius Naso on the Inci-
      dence of Sex in the Contemporary Novel   21

La Foce   22

Old Man's Journey   23

Tyrant of Syracuse   24

Where a Poet's From 25

Mark's Sheep 26

Cummings 27

Hemingway 28

Edwin Muir 29

William Adams Delano 30

Rue Carpenter 31

Brooks Atkinson 32

April in November 34

How the River Ninfa Runs Through the
    Ruined Town Beneath the Lime Quarry 35

Contemporary Portrait 37

Pity's Sake 38

November 39

Hotel Breakfast 40

Rainbow at Evening 41

Arrival and Departure 42

Late Abed 43

"The Wild Old Wicked Man" 44

"THE WILD OLD WICKED MAN"
& OTHER POEMS

HURRICANE

Sleep at noon. Window blind
rattle and bang. Pay no mind.
Door go jump like somebody coming:
let him come. Tin roof drumming:
drum away — she's drummed before.
Blinds blow loose: unlatch the door.
Look up sky through the manchineel:
black show through like a hole in your heel.
Look down shore at the old canoe:
rag-a-tag sea turn white, turn blue,
kick up dust in the lee of the reef,
wallop around like a loblolly leaf.
Let her wallop — who's afraid?
Gale from the north-east: just the Trade . . .

And that's when you hear it: far and high —
sea-birds screaming down the sky
high and far like screaming leaves;
tree-branch slams across the eaves;
rain like pebbles on the ground . . .

and the sea turns white and the wind goes round.

THE SHIP IN THE TOMB

Cheops, to sail eternity,
built him a ship, a real one, sea-
worthy, solid cedar, gear
complete to the last metaphor;

even a heavy-weather prow
to breast the spiritual surge and throw
the foam of fiery stars about.
Cheops was wise. He knew. Without

the shape of actual ship the notion
founders in that kind of ocean.

Consider the Idea of God. Before
God was God forevermore
how was immortality made known?
By stone.

Even the Idea must start
in stone, surmount the stone by art,
surmount the art by Angelo,
leave Angelo upon his Sistine ceiling . . .
and so
   go.

Even the Idea demands
the work of hands,
the shape to feel.

CREATOR

The world was made by someone else,
not God. The moist, inexplicable bees,
the crystal stones, the painted shells,
the lights beyond the swarming Pleiades —

God knows nothing of these things.
We found him in the burning bush
above the desert where he sings
as flames do, trilling in their fiery hush.

He told us where the end was, knew
the way to reach it, showed the path:
there men like marigolds, he said, come true
and understand their lives and live their death.

We help each other through the blind
tall night beneath the infinite spaces:
God looks before and we behind
but somewhere else that other unknown face is.

THE BOATMEN OF SANTORIN

The boatmen on the bay of Santorin
where the world blew up about the time of Minos
sit with their hands on their oars inviting the tourists.

Visit the myth! Visit the fable!
Visit the drowned volcano where the world
blew up about the time of Minos!

The sea sings. The sun shines.
Visit the end of the world! they shout to you.

And all at once on the bright blue
tourist sea, suds of pumice,
floating shoals of grey decaying stone,
grate at the wooden oars.

We float here
feathering death at our oar-blades.

THE PEEPERS IN OUR MEADOW

The way at night these piping peepers
suddenly and all at once are still —
too suddenly, too all together, to have dropped asleep
at God's sweet will.

Things stop like that: altogether.
Nations falter, great art fails,
ages of poetry draw Periclean breath;
then death prevails.

What stills these peepers in our midnight pond?
Do wings go over? Skulkers come?
Or are they silenced by that silence out beyond?
Struck dumb?

WAKING

The sadness we bring back from sleep
like an herb in the mouth . . .
> sage?
> > rosemary?

like a fragrance we can neither lose nor
keep . . .
> woodsmoke?
> > oak-leaves?

like the closing
softly of a distant . . .
> distant? . . .
> > door . . .

> > > Oh
like earth on our shoes from an unremembered journey . . .
What earth?
> What journey?

> > Why did we return?

AUTOBIOGRAPHY

There was a landscape in my childhood
over opposite — against:
another world than this one, wild
and hence.

There was another time, an earliness:
the sun came up out of Eden, out of the Odyssey —
freshness like the fragrance of a girl
or god.

What do I know of the mystery of the universe?
Only the mystery — that there was a mystery:
something opposite beneath the moon
to this.

But I who saw it — who was I?
And who am I who say this to you? All
I know now of that world, that time,
is false.

REVOLUTION OF THE CHILDREN

Leafless Dodder, Rabbit's Silk,
wind-sown on some farmer's acre,
cut for fodder, fed for milk,
crazes a city's children. Sómething
odder, dafter, dizzier than cow
sniggers in the school-bus laughter,
capers at the picture show,
when Leafless Dodder, Rabbit's Silk,
scents the city's sanitary milk.

Girls in scants and boys in beards
offer to make love to flowers,
Jesus dances, music showers,
words and weirds sing songs together,
heifers in their lolling herds
leave the green alfalfa, feed
on gossamer of Rabbit's Silk,
on thistle down of Dodder seed.

Let ordinances close the town
to Dodder seed, that thistle down,
to gossamer of Rabbit's Silk —
there'll still
                be milk.

BLACK HUMOR

The jangle of the jeering crows
has somehow crossed into my dream
to scream and circle there. I seem
in sleep to understand the crows.

Evil is in the world, they scream.
Something on the garden path
salt as blood and cold as death
has fallen from the air, the dream.

I find it with the daylight, too:
cold upon the path, to gather
drops of silence from the dew,
one inscrutable, black, bleeding feather.

BOY IN THE ROMAN ZOO

TO THE FLAMINGOS

               Ravished arms,
delighted eyes — and all the rest,
parental cautions and alarms,
treacherous sidewalks and his best
blue suit forgotten. He has seen
heaven upon the further shore
and nothing in the null between
has mere existence anymore.
Those shapes of rose, those coals of ice,
command him as love never has
and only they can now suffice.
Forgotten is the child he was,
unguessed the man he will be. One
moment, free of both, he'll run
toward the flamingos in the sun.

SEEING

(1)
By Night

What did you see, Cromarty, by the house
or where the house once was?

A tree.

I know it hurts. I have to ask you.

I said I saw a tree.

What kind of
tree?

A pear tree.

Look here, soldier!
Look! We drop a flare. You see . . .
what do you see?

A pear. A tree . . .

I told you I was sorry . . .

. . . tree
bloom in the night.

And that was all?

No. I saw a petal fall.

Think! You haven't long, Cromarty.

I thought! Good God, I thought! I thought,
Christ! I'd never seen a tree!

And that was all . . . ?

(2)
At the Saturday Club

Harlow: Our generation discovered the universe.

Robert: That's why we're lost.

Harlow: Men before us
thought in beginnings and ends, all of them.
Nobody knew that time is a circle,
that space is a circle, that space-time
closes the circle.

Robert: They weren't lost.

Harlow: They didn't know they were lost but they were:
they were wrong.

Robert: And we're right and we're lost.

Harlow: When you're right
        you can't be lost: you know where you are.

Robert: You know where you are when you're lost.

Harlow: Where?

Robert: Lost.

(3)
In the East

Why are you moving your lips, said the Emperor I Tsung.

I am blessing the prophets, said Ibn Wahab the traveler.

Where are the prophets, said the Emperor I Tsung.
        I do not see them.

You see them, said Ibn Wahab the traveler:
        you do not recognize them but you see them.

I see a man in a boat on a great ocean, said the Emperor I
        Tsung.

That, said Ibn Wahab the traveler, is Jesus.
            who swam on the world when the Flood drowned it.

I see a man in the fields, said the Emperor I Tsung:
            he is wandering.

That is Abraham, said Ibn Wahab the traveler:
            he is wandering everywhere looking for God.

I see a man on a tree, said the Emperor I Tsung.

That, said Ibn Wahab the traveler, is Jesus.

What did he do, said the Emperor I Tsung:
            did he swim on the world? Did he wander everywhere?

He died, said Ibn Wahab the traveler.

Why do I weep, said the Emperor I Tsung.

You have recognized Jesus, said Ibn Wahab the traveler.

(4)
At the Dark's Edge

Sister tree,
deaf and dumb and blind, and we
have ears to hear, have eyes for sight,
and yet our sister tree can find,
fumbling deaf and groping blind,
the field before her and the wood behind,
what we can't . . .
$$\text{light.}$$

COMPANIONS

The flowers with the ragged names,
daffodils and such,
met us on the road we came,
nodded, touched.

Now, the golden day gone by,
we walk the other road:
they throng the evening grass beside,
touch us . . .
                    nod.

SURVIVOR

On an oak in autumn
there'll always be
one leaf left at the top of the tree
that won't let go with the rest and rot —
won't cast loose and skitter and sail
and end in a puddle of rain in a swale
and fatten the earth and be fruitful . . .
No,
it won't and it won't and it won't let go.
It rattles a kind of a jig tattoo,
a telegrapher's tattle that *will* get through
like an SOS from a struggling ship
over and over, a dash and a skip.

You cover your head with your quilt and still
that telegrapher's key on Conway hill
calls to Polaris.

I can spell:
I know what it says . . . I know too well.
I pull my pillow over my ear
but I hear.

GREAT CONTEMPORARY DISCOVERIES

The Writers: We die.

The Readers: Aie!

The Writers: We disappear from the
                  bed, the bedroom, from the chair:
                  nothing remembers us.

The Readers: Perhaps a mirror
                  found on a closet shelf long afterward? —
                  Whose? Hers? Tinkle of memory . . . ?

The Writers: We leave no memory.

The Readers: A son? A daughter?

The Writers: They too die, one first then the other:
                  the house sold, the furniture carted off,
                  different flowers.

The Readers: God then: God will remember us.

The Writers: How can God remember us? Think of the
                  earth, that boneyard — a man's tooth by a
                     jackal's —
                  Olduvai of indistinguishable bones!

The Readers: Nevertheless we have lived. We leave our lives.

The Writers: What is a man's life! An absurdity —
　　　　　　extinguished unintelligible cry.

The Readers: Absurd? Our lives?

The Writers: 　　　　　　　　　Because we die.

The Readers: But Sirs! But Sirs! That's why we love them.

The Writers: 　　　　　　　　　　　　Why?

The Readers: Because we die!

The Writers: 　　　　　　Aie!

SPRING IN THESE HILLS

Slow May
deliberate in the peach tree,
lighting the pear blossoms, one first then another,
sullen almost sometimes,
comes,
delicately through the thaws of snow
to scatter
daffodils like drifting flaws
of sunlight on these winter hills.

OBSERVATIONS OF P. OVIDIUS NASO
ON THE INCIDENCE OF SEX IN THE
CONTEMPORARY NOVEL

What have they done to you, all-conquering love? —
you who taught the lecherous birds to preen and even
men to walk like men for pride of love —
what have they done to you?

                    And who are these,
these nudest, lewdest, noisiest, their naked buttocks
scarcely skirted and their breasts tipped up to tease —
these who set upon you with their silver scissors,
clip your famous arrow, cut
your bowstring, tell you what your mother is
and walk off whistling?

                    Show me, you,
all-conquering triumphant captain, what
precisely you propose to do!

LA FOCE

Close the shutters. Let the ceiling fly
dance around the chandelier
in silent circles with inaudible small cry
in celebration of my seventieth year.

Why grow older in a Tuscan spring
where everything,
follies and flowers, loves and leaves,
grows younger and the loam conceives
and even the slow venerable sun
splashes in the water spills
and hills
invent again the new
first blue?

Close the shutters. Tuscan noon.
A hen upon the barley ground
tells the welkin what her industry has found
and heaven answers. All must run,
Yeats tells us, backward to be new begun
as does the silver bullion of the moon.

Only one small circling fly
remembers that the world goes by
and we go with it
                    he and I.

OLD MAN'S JOURNEY

The deep-sea salmon far at sea,
fierce with silver, scoured with salt,
flailing toward eternity,
returns as we do — our too human fault.

Remembrance of the brown Tobique,
the gravel shoal, the succulent mud,
the inchling sleepers cheek to cheek
somehow infects his restless blood,

and seasons after, in the deep,
cold, farthest ocean flood, he sees
the pebbled rift, the pools of sleep,
the rippling shallows under rippling trees,

and turns and puts his journey by
and climbs from sea to stream to brook to die.

Only in Dante's Hell does Ulysses
sail on and on to always farther seas.

TYRANT OF SYRACUSE

This stranger in my blood, my skin,
can I command him? Will he stand
when I say stand? Come out? Go in?
Do anything?
                    And yet if he,
snake in his brittle grass, command
I jump I tell you! Haw or Gee
I take his orders, come awake
when he wakes, sleep when he sleeps, love
what pleases him and for his sake
not mine. He's master, lord thereof,
Tyrant of Syracuse who hears
whatever's spoken in the cave.
                              Sometimes,
pacing the silence in a fit of work,
a half-made poem humming in my ears,
hammering its pattern in my mind,
I'll know he's listening in that room behind,
stirring a little in his place to smirk
and nod as though he'd shaped the rhymes . . .

he! that fumbler! dumb and blind!

WHERE A POET'S FROM

Where he's born?
Settles? Where the papers claim him?
Carl Sandburg, born in Illinois,
died in Flat Rock, Carolina, in Chicago famous —

where was Sandburg from? Chicago?
People knew where Frost was from
in spite of San Francisco — from New England.
What town or what proud county knew this other coming?

He lived around: he lived in Kansas,
Chicago on the Old West Side,
Michigan, Nebraska — in Wisconsin.
Where was Carl from in the Carolinas when he died?

His tongue might tell: he talked "Peoria" —
O as in Oh or Low, the way
the railroad trainmen on the Illinois
called it in those cool reverberating stations.

His sound might say: he said "Missouri" —
a stumbled M and an S and an OO
long as a night freight off across the prairie
asking the moon for answers and the sound goes through and
    through.

Where was Sandburg from, old poet,
dead in Carolina in his great repute?
"Peoria," he said, "Missouri," the neglected names
that now, because his mouth has spoken them, are beautiful.

MARK'S SHEEP

Mark's sheep, I said, but they were only
stones, boulders in the uncropped grass,
granite shoulders weathered to the bone
and old as that first morning where God was.

And yet they looked like sheep — so like
you half expected them to startle,
bolt in a leap because some tyke
had barked, because a bluejay darted —

dart of shadow under blue of jay —
or someone shouted by the water trough,
slammed a car-door, drove away,
or squirrels quarreled, or a gun went off,

or just because they must: that terrified
impulse to be somewhere else
browsers and ruminators seem to share
as though they knew, they only, the sky falls

and *here* is dangerous (as of course it is).
But Mark's sheep never startled from the grass.
They knew their place, their boulders' business:
to let the nights go over, the days pass,

let years go, summer, autumn, winter,
each by itself, each motionless, alone,
praising the world by being in it,
praising the earth by being stone.

CUMMINGS

"He was sitting watching the sunset."
                    Marion Cummings, September 2, 1962

True
poet who could live and die
eye to eye

The rain ends, the sky slides
east a little as our skies here do
this time of year and lets the sunset through . . .

or not the sunset either but a blue
between the hill and what the cloud still hides
that promises
                    a poet's blue

I should have known, my friend, you'd watch it too
eastward across New Hampshire where the night
found you in that glimpse of light

The cloud lifts and the rift of blue
blazes and the sun comes through

HEMINGWAY

"In some inexplicable way an accident."
                                    Mary Hemingway

Oh, not inexplicable. Death explains,
that kind of death: rewinds remembrance
backward like a film track till the laughing man
among the lilacs, peeling the green stem,
waits for the gunshot where the play began;

rewinds those Africas and Idahos and Spains
to find the table at the Closerie des Lilas,
sticky with syrup, where the flash of joy
flamed into blackness like that flash of steel.

The gun between the teeth explains.
The shattered mouth foretells the singing boy.

EDWIN MUIR

The memory of Edwin Muir is green
as garden parsley when the first hard frost
blackens the asters and the rose is lost —
snow in all the garden paths between.

"Strophe of small leaves
in the inevitable spiral,
versicle of God . . ."

still lyre.

Aie, how they sang in their youth together,
trill of Hesiod in the spring,
Pindar in the showery weather,
all those lovely poets . . .
                                how they sing!

WILLIAM ADAMS DELANO

The supple haft, the helve,
outlasts the brutal stick.

The brittle honey wax
outburns the tallow wick.

The man with ardor quick,
the man by grace refined,

though girth and thew he lack
and live but by the mind

can still outcount by twelve
the Grand Climacteric

and where the great decay
and where the gross decline

grow nobler day by day:
reveal the pure design.

RUE CARPENTER

Some for their looks,
some for their powers,
some like Rue Carpenter
for bowls of flowers.

Some for an age,
some a few hours,
some like Rue Carpenter
as long as flowers.

BROOKS ATKINSON

Brooks Atkinson, that quiet man
who kept the torches of Parnassus
steady as New England can
(or could) behind his steel-rimmed glasses,

Brooks Atkinson who loved the tongue
well consonanted and well voweled
(Actors who mouthed it should be hung,
writers who blurred it, disemboweled),

Brooks Atkinson who hated hue
and cry and mode and art-in-fashion,
and never wrote a wrong review
to show his wit or wave his passion

or imitate the *dernier cri*
or scratch for academic plaudit
but saw the plays there were to see
and searched his soul and made his audit

and kept alive for thirty years
of Venus in a pouting sweater,
Ares in skirts and art in tears,
the taste for good, the hope for better,

Brooks Atkinson, the role complete,
the task performed, the judgment certain,

prepared to vanish from his seat
unnoticed at the final curtain.

Wrong for once. The faithful man
who guards the honor of the muses
never vanishes, never can:
they keep his fame for their sweet uses.

APRIL IN NOVEMBER

Even in spring, even in first
spring when the tree can put forth again
mending its broken branches with new green,
even in spring there is ruin enough from these tempests,
whirling tornadoes from God knows where, violent and
unforetellable sudden descent of the wind on the
white leaves and the gasp and the branches threshing . . .

Unwished, unexpected visit of loveliness.

Now, this later season of the year
there is no healing green, the bare
bole stands broken for the world to see.

Unseasonable tempest: naked tree.

34

HOW THE RIVER NINFA RUNS THROUGH THE RUINED TOWN BENEATH THE LIME QUARRY

to remember Marguerite Caetani

Italy breaking her bones for bread
eating her stones

But the Nymph, O the Nymph in her crisp cresses
clattering over the cobbles on slippery
heels where the little palazzi were and the churches
ages ago, ages ago . . .

O but the Nymph in her cool cresses
jigging with midges in the slants of sun
nobody's shadow now, nobody's shadow . . .

chattering under the bridges nobody's shoes . . .

O but the Nymph in her crisp cresses
cracking her knuckles in time with a tune
nobody knows anymore now, nobody . . .

chuckling her fables
over and over again and then
when the dynamite kicks at the sky and the quarry . . .

Italy breaking her bones for bread
eating her stones

. . . shudders and tumbles . . .

O but the Nymph! — how she hushes and humbles
just for a heart's beat and is dumb . . .

. . . Nymph in the ruin of time . . .

and then laughs again.

CONTEMPORARY PORTRAIT

This woman mask that wears her to the bone
they say for certain is her soul's disguise:
such holes are cut in colored cloth for eyes
where the live lid winks beneath the painted one.

The eyes are hers, the mouth is not her own.
The mouth smiles soft, remembers well, complies,
laughs, lifts a little, kisses — these are lies
when at the lid the tragic look is shown.

Whether her soul in fear has made this mask
for easier wandering beneath our moon
or time has tricked her so, they never ask:
they know the false face hides the honest one.

And yet it's certain, when she comes to die,
this is the face that death will know her by.

PITY'S SAKE

For pity's sake
never give the heart away!
Sell it, barter it for marbles, play
the ponies with it, let it break,
but never give the heart away
for pity's sake.

When pity gives what pride should take
love becomes a hand to hold,
a comfortable knee, a shoulder
made to cry on in the cold
and by and by
a nastier falsehood than a lie.

Go out, my dear, too old to play,
but never give the heart away
for pity's sake.

NOVEMBER

A drop on the window, once, twice.
A blasted rose at the end of a brier.
Sparrows in the weeds like mice
and the cat indoors beside the fire.

Love, old love and old desire,
let the puddles skin with ice;
pile the bed up higher, higher . . .

Time at the window, once, twice.

HOTEL BREAKFAST

On a stale morning
in a miserable winter town in Illinois
neither of us ever heard of,

sipping a sticky cup of some
(not tea, not coffee, cocoa?) tepid brew
you surely, of all living, never knew,

the napkin reeking of its dead cigars
(scent of yellow roses was your warning),
suddenly,
        across the table,
                you.

The plastic prisms of the chandelier
shiver with laughter from another year,
another country, Oh, another life;
the cold sun crawls along the butter knife.

I tremble, heartsick with a mortal fear —

What brings you here?

RAINBOW AT EVENING

Rainbow over evening, my
Iris of the after-sky,
show me, now the gales are by,
where the gold is.
                    When the rain
crazed the whirling weather vane
I never wondered. I knew then.
Gold was where the heart could find.

Now the heart is out of mind
in this late light your seal has signed,
show me, *arc-en-ciel*, bright bow,
where the gold is hidden now.

ARRIVAL AND DEPARTURE

The train slows down,
  the town appears,
    persons in
the *Place 'la Gare*
  sit in Sunday
    hats and stare,

Sunday sunshine
  stalks the cats.
    The engine sighs.
Across the square
  a window opens:
    heavy hair

Falls all gold
  from sill to air.
    The engine jerks,
the *Place* withdraws,
  the staring faces
    turn away.

(They go: we stay.)

  The window opens:
    heavy hair
falls all gold
  from sill to air . . .

  Our journey to the
world stopped there.

LATE ABED

Ah, but a good wife!
To lie late in a warm bed
(warm where she was) with your life
suspended like a music in the head,
hearing her foot in the house, her broom
on the pine floor of the down-stairs room,
hearing the window toward the sun go up,
the tap turned on, the tap turned off,
the saucer clatter to the coffee cup . . .

To lie late in the odor of coffee
thinking of nothing at all, listening . . .

and she moves here, she moves there,
and your mouth hurts still where last she kissed you:
you think how she looked as she left, the bare
thigh, and went to her adorning . . .

You lie there listening and she moves —
prepares her house to hold another morning,
prepares another day to hold her loves . . .

You lie there
thinking of nothing
watching the sky . . .

"THE WILD OLD WICKED MAN"

Too old for love and still to love! —
Yeats's predicament and mine — all men's:
the aging Adam who must strut and shove
and caper his obscene pretense . . .

And yet, within the dry thorn grove,
singer to singer in the dusk, there cries
(Listen! Ah, listen, the wood dove!)
something conclusion never satisfies;

and still when day ends and the wind goes down
and not a tree stirs, not a leaf,
some passion in the sea beats on
and on . . .
             (Oh, listen, the sea reef!)

Too old for love and still to long . . .
for what? For one more flattering proof
the flesh lives and the beast is strong? —
once more upon the pulse that hammering hoof?

Or is there something the persistent dove,
the ceaseless surges and the old man's lust
all know and cannot say? Is love

what nothing concludes, nothing must,
pure certainty?

And does the passionate man
most nearly know it when no passion can?
Is this the old man's triumph, to pursue
impossibility — and take it too?